PRACTICAL STOICISM

Exercises for Doing the Right Thing Right Now

Version 2.3.2

By Grey Freeman

©*2017 - 2021 Grey Freeman*

This work is licensed under the Creative Commons Attribution-NonCommercial-ShareAlike 4.0 International License. To view a copy of this license, visit http://creativecommons.org/licenses/by-nc-sa/4.0/.

'The Acropolis' (1846) by Leo von Klenze is in the public domain in its country of origin and other countries and areas where the copyright term is the author's life plus 100 years or less.

Dedication

To Bruce, who got it. And proved it.

"Knowing is not enough, we must apply. Willing is not enough, we must do." – Bruce Lee

Contents

Dedication 3

Contents 4

Foreword 7

Get Up 10

Catch a Sunrise 12

Prepare for Battle 13

Review Your Impressions 16

Brace for Trolls 18

Ready Your Tools 20

Pause, Assess, Then Decide 21

Apply the Fork 23

Use Your Head 26

Take a 3rd-Party Perspective 29

Support Your Community 31

Consider Worst Case Scenarios 33

Retreat into the Self 36

Choose Your Company Well 39

Use Self-Deprecating Humor ... 41

Let the Other Guy Talk ... 43

Live Simply ... 45

Speak Without Judging ... 48

Educate by Example ... 50

Practice Discomfort ... 53

Seek Your Own Approval ... 55

Enjoy the Silence ... 58

Hold On Loosely ... 60

Renounce ... 63

Focus on the Thing at Hand ... 65

Master Your Appetite ... 68

Break It Down ... 71

Emulate Your Role Models ... 74

Turn It Around ... 77

Take a View from Above ... 79

Own It ... 81

Walk in Your Enemy's Shoes ... 83

Nail Your Part ... 86

Reconsider the Wrong 89

Police Your Thoughts 92

Amor Fati 94

Write It Down 97

Memento Mori 99

Review the Day 101

A Final Word 103

Acknowledgements 105

Appendix: Companion Material 106

About the Author 110

Foreword

'So, how exactly does one actually do this 'Stoic' thing?" - Multiple posters on r/stoicism

Much has been written on the topic of what Stoics believe, and why, but that merely sets the table for what truly matters: The actual application of the philosophy. Because it is far too easy to continually educate and ruminate and contemplate without actually doing anything useful, I want to help minimize the gap between thought and action as much as possible by providing a short guide of practical things one can actually *do* to bring one's philosophy out of the world of the theoretical into the moment where we actually live.

A note on the presentation: I have broken this book into several small essays of about a "page" (depending on how you are reading it) apiece - one per practice. Each practice begins with a verb. It's important to understand that these are things you "do", even if it's all happening in your head. This is not a dissertation on theory.

This book is not a primer for the new initiate. Consider it more as a companion piece, to be read alongside other works that go further into the reasoning behind the practices discussed here. Without that component, this becomes a collection of empty ritual. Without this, those might lead you to believe that reading something inspirational is akin to doing something useful (*See the "*Companion Material*" appendix for suggestions.*)

Read these pages on random. The book is intended to be consumed in small bites, whenever one is idle or feeling off true, to act as a goad to do the thing that needs to be done. Contemplate a practice and consider if it seems helpful to you. And, if so, how you might integrate it into your life. Then do it. As Bruce says, "Knowing is not enough".

Now I know a refuge never grows

From a chin in a hand in a thoughtful pose

Gotta tend the earth if you want a rose

Emily Saliers

Get Up

At dawn, when you have trouble getting out of bed, tell yourself: 'I have to go to work—as a human being. What do I have to complain of, if I'm going to do what I was born for—the things I was brought into the world to do? Or is this what I was created for? To huddle under the blankets and stay warm?'

—But it's nicer here...

So you were born to feel 'nice'? Instead of doing things and experiencing them? Don't you see the plants, the birds, the ants and spiders and bees going about their individual tasks, putting the world in order, as best they can? And you're not willing to do your job as a human being? Why aren't you running to do what your nature demands? (Marcus Aurelius, Meditations V.1)

Like almost everything else in life, more than enough sleep is too much. Studies show that sleeping more than an average of 7-8 hours a day can lead to diabetes, obesity, headaches, back pain, and heart disease. What's worse, and more immediate, is that any hour spent sleeping beyond what your body actually needs to recuperate or repair itself is an hour you have lost forever.

An hour lost to sleep will not be available to you for meditation. That hour cannot be used to make you stronger and more resilient. It cannot be used to make the world a better place. In that hour, you will not test yourself and grow. You will do no great deeds in that hour. You will not even remember it happened. It is simply buried, eternally, beneath the sands of time. An irreplaceable treasure lost to the ages.

Better to take back the hour and use it as your nature demands. You've rested enough. Time now to take a deep breath and get on with living your life.

Catch a Sunrise

The Pythagoreans bid us in the morning look to the heavens that we may be reminded of those bodies that continually do the same things and in the same manner perform their work, and also be reminded of their purity and nudity. For there is no veil over a star. (Marcus Aurelius, Meditations XI.27)

Every once in the while, find the time to get out of bed before sunrise and drag yourself to where you can see it. It doesn't take that long and it's a magnificent sight. Think of your place in the universe. Consider that, whatever you've done before, here is one more chance to get it right.

There are no guarantees you'll see another one. Use this opportunity wisely.

Prepare for Battle

"Cling tooth and nail to the following rule: Not to give in to adversity, never to trust prosperity, and always to take full note of fortune's habit of behaving just as she pleases, treating her as if she were actually going to do everything it is in her power to do. Whatever you have been expecting for some time comes as less of a shock." (Seneca, Letters from a Stoic)

One way (of several) to do the *"Premeditatio Malorum"*, the "premeditation of evils", is to start your day with a walk through your calendar. Consider what you will do, where you will go, and who you will meet. Imagine how it might go wrong.

Now, think about how it will feel. How it will look to others. How you might be embarrassed, or angered, or disappointed. Just this part of the exercise has its benefits. It deadens the pain of the actual event, if it actually happens, through a sort of emotional-hardening process.

It even extends to other, unrelated events - If you can endure sorrow better in *this* instance, you can endure it elsewhere.

Now consider how you might respond to this misfortune. How you might lessen the damage, soften the blow. Use this as an opportunity to do a little contingency planning. If the presentation goes poorly, is there another resource you can appeal to? Can you repurpose the meeting advantageously? Can you lay the groundwork for a second attempt?

Extend your definition of "misfortune" to include diversions and temptations that might challenge your values. Determine ahead of time how you will handle the free doughnuts in the break room. That cute married lady who flirts with you. That guy who is always making fun of your co-workers.

Finally, consider how you will handle the undesired emotions. How will you maintain the space you need to form a reasoned response?

Just thinking about it lessens the shock. Knowing your strengths and weaknesses, what else are you going to have to do?

Now you can start the day knowing that you can still be surprised, but you can't be shaken.

Review Your Impressions

So make a practice at once of saying to every strong impression: 'An impression is all you are, not the source of the impression.' Then test and assess it with your criteria, but one primarily: ask, 'Is this something that is, or is not, in my control?' And if it's not one of the things that you control, be ready with the reaction, 'Then it's none of my concern.' (Epictetus, Enchiridion I.5)

Review your recent emotional responses. What made you angry? What nagging fear continues to wear at you? To whom do you have antipathy? In short, what negative emotions are you experiencing? Now ask yourself "why?" If virtue is sufficient for fulfillment, why are you feeling anything other than serenity? To what inappropriate impression have you assented? What virtue have you lacked to allow this disharmony into your "inner citadel"?

If there is an area of particular concern, start keeping a count of those incidents when it has raised its ugly head. Often, just measuring a thing goes a long way towards fixing it. Just knowing that, for instance, you lost your cool and yelled at the teenager four times this week. Or that you snacked twice when you'd promised yourself you wouldn't. It's not a judgment, it's just a number. But there are reasons behind the number, and you can work with those.

Brace for Trolls

Say to yourself in the early morning: I shall meet today inquisitive, ungrateful, violent, treacherous, envious, uncharitable men. All these things have come upon them through ignorance of real good and ill. People do not choose to behave the way they do so that men of a certain type should behave as they do is inevitable. To wish it otherwise were to wish the fig-tree would not yield its juice. (Marcus Aurelius, Meditations II.1)

As pessimistic as it sounds, one can't deny the truth of it: On any given day, you will meet a few jerks. Similarly to "Prepare for Battle", it's best to anticipate that and remove the sting of surprise.

But further, consider how you will handle them, philosophically. Go through the mental play-acting of not losing your cool, of acknowledging that they could only act as they do. Consider how you will preserve your serenity and remain above the fray. Admit that you have your faults, too, and sometimes you hide them better than other times.

Imagine that, somewhere in your fine city, someone else is taking a deep breath, making a face, and preparing to deal with *you*.

Ready Your Tools

As physicians have always their instruments and knives ready for cases that suddenly require their skill, so do you have principles ready for the understanding of things divine and human, and for doing everything, even the smallest, with a recollection of the bond that unites the divine and human to each other. (Marcus Aurelius, Meditations III.13)

Have memorized those guide-posts you find most helpful in your philosophy. Quotes, maxims, the basics of your belief system - whatever it takes to bring you back to center. Keep copies of *Meditations*, *The Enchiridion*, and whatever else you find inspirational and supportive to your practice (even this thing) close to hand. Review them regularly so that you can recall the right response with minimal effort.

A *caveat*: Preparing your tools should never be used as an excuse to not use them. You can spend so much time getting ready to live that you never get around to actually living. Ready them, but don't wait for them.

The easier it is to access those guiding principles you have chosen to follow, the easier it is to find the right tools when you face your next challenge.

Pause, Assess, Then Decide

Remember, it is not enough to be hit or insulted to be harmed, you must believe that you are being harmed. If someone succeeds in provoking you, realize that your mind is complicit in the provocation. Which is why it is essential that we not respond impulsively to impressions; take a moment before reacting, and you will find it is easier to maintain control. (Epictetus, Enchiridion XX)

Whenever you are assailed with a powerful emotional reaction, immediately take a deep breath and separate the event from your impression of it. The event is what happened; your "impression" is how you have, initially, instinctively viewed it. Will you assent?

Anything outside your control is of no real concern. It cannot touch the *you* that matters. But your considered response is, indeed, yours to control. Will you choose to be angry? Depressed? Afraid? Why? How do those things help you? How do they make you stronger or more virtuous? How do they lead to a life of *eudemonia*?

Instead, take a deep breath and reach for some perspective. Whatever it was that happened, it's already drifting into the past. What does *this* moment require of you?

Apply the Fork

Of all existing things some are in our power, and others are not in our power. In our power are thought, impulse, will to get and will to avoid, and, in a word, everything which is our own doing. Things not in our power include the body, property, reputation, office, and, in a word, everything which is not our own doing. Things in our power are by nature free, unhindered, untrammelled; things not in our power are weak, servile, subject to hindrance, dependent on others. Remember then that if you imagine that what is naturally slavish is free, and what is naturally another's is your own, you will be hampered, you will mourn, you will be put to confusion, you will blame gods and men; but if you think that only your own belongs to you, and that what is another's is indeed another's, no one will ever put compulsion or hindrance on you, you will blame none, you will accuse none, you will do nothing against your will, no one will harm you, you will have no enemy, for no harm can touch you. (Epictetus, Enchiridion I)

In all things that you believe to concern you, you must apply the Stoic Fork: "Is this thing within my power?"

Things that occur in your head, those impressions to which you assent, the actions you undertake, the thoughts you form, and the exercise of your will – these you control completely. No external force can make you do any of these, nor stop you from doing them.

But the results of your efforts are largely *not* under your control. You can do everything right and prudent and still not be rewarded. You can study extensively and still be considered a fool. You can work like a mule and still be poor. You can live a healthy lifestyle and still get sick.

The classic Stoic example is that of the archer. The archer can take the correct stance, aim perfectly, and release the arrow with precision. But anything can happen after that. The wind can change and blow the arrow off target. The target can move. The string could break.

None of these results should matter if the archer restricts his concern to performing his task well. It is the effort put forth, the intent, the will that matters, because we control it. If you restrict your concern to that which you control, and you address those concerns with wisdom and courage, you will be fulfilled.

Or you can chase after things outside your control and forever be a slave to the whims of fate.

Use Your Head

I am content if I am in accord with Nature in what I will to get and will to avoid, if I follow Nature in impulse to act and to refrain from action, in purpose, and design and assent. (Epictetus, Discourses XXII)

At its very core, the font from which all other Stoic teaching spring is "Follow nature". This is not a command to hug trees and dance with the satyrs, but to act in the manner that naturally allows us to flourish. These principals work because they are natural. Every law in the universe supports them and, like gravity, any attempt to ignore them will have unfortunate consequences.

One can understand the Stoic discipline of "Ethics" as being the study of *how* to correctly follow nature. To do this, one must have a solid grasp of the "Logic" discipline. And the information to which one applies that logic comes from the final discipline, Physics. The ancient Stoics understood Physics as a combination of what we would today refer to as natural science, metaphysics, and theology. More broadly, it can simply be understood as, "the way things are".

Following nature means following the facts. It means getting the facts about the physical and social world we inhabit, and the facts about our situation in it-our own powers, relationships, limitations, possibilities, motives, intentions, and endeavors before we deliberate about normative matters. (Lawrence Becker, A New Stoicism)

So, you use Logic to understand Physics, which tells you what is Ethical. Put another way, you use reason to study facts in order to figure out what to do. Or how to live.

If you understand this process, then you'll recognize that all the other teachings of the ancients are simply rules of thumb derived from the *first* rule: To follow nature. In any situation where find yourself at a loss concerning what is "right", if your maxims are in conflict, if you forget what Epictetus said about it, if the "rules" are counter-intuitive, your default response should always be to fall back to the source and "follow nature".

And that just means, "Use your head." If the facts change, you adjust. If you don't have enough information, you get more. If your current path doesn't make sense, you go a different direction. "Use only that which works, and take it from any place you can find it."

There is no "orthodoxy" in a living philosophy, and you can't be doing it wrong if you're making it work.

Take a 3rd-Party Perspective

We can familiarize ourselves with the will of nature by calling to mind our common experiences. When a friend breaks a glass, we are quick to say, 'Oh, bad luck.' It's only reasonable, then, that when a glass of your own breaks, you accept it in the same patient spirit. Moving on to graver things: when somebody's wife or child dies, to a man we all routinely say, 'Well, that's part of life.' But if one of our own family is involved, then right away it's 'Poor, poor me!' We would do better to remember how we react when a similar loss afflicts others. (Epictetus, Enchiridion XXVI)

If you hear that your neighbor has a busted water heater, do you sympathetically worry that he will go broke dealing with it? Most likely, you take it with a shrug and figure he'll work it out with no significant impact on his lifestyle. But at your own house, the possibility of a significant home repair bill is cause for great concern. Is it because your neighbor is more capable than you?

It's natural, but not reasonable, to feel like your challenges are of greater import than those encountered by others. They're simply closer. To get a more objective perspective, it's often helpful to take a step back and view your obstacles as if you were a disinterested, but sympathetic, 3rd party. Would someone in that role be concerned for you? Or would they see the situation as one of the sort that people encounter daily, and daily navigate without injury?

It's hard to justify an emotional reaction to a situation that is only important because it's happening to you.

Support Your Community

If mind is common to us, then also the reason, whereby we are reasoning beings, is common. If this be so, then also the reason which enjoins what is to be done or left undone is common. If this be so, law also is common; if this be so, we are citizens; if this be so, we are partakers in one constitution; if this be so, the Universe is a kind of Commonwealth. (Marcus Aurelius, Meditations IV:5)

Again, they [the Stoics] hold that the universe is governed by divine will; it is a city or state of which both men and gods are members, and each one of us is a part of this universe from which it is a natural consequence that we should prefer the common advantage to our own. (Cicero, De Finibus)

One must consider that, in a certain way, one's brothers are parts of oneself, just as my eyes are parts of me and so too my legs and hands and the rest. (Hierocles, Fragments and Excerpts)

The Stoic concept of *oikeiosis* posits that a stoic should steadily increase the scope of his concerns to include the wellbeing of not just himself, not just his family, and not just the nation but all of humanity. They considered this an extension of the foundational motto, *"The goal of life is to live in agreement with nature"*, because it is natural for any animal, as it matures, to look towards the preservation of the species. So, too, should we, if we are to mature.

What can you do to aid in the preservation of your species? What can you do to treat your fellow humans as if they were citizens of your universal Commonwealth, your brothers, your arms?

Start by thinking of them that way.

Consider Worst Case Scenarios

"We should remind our spirits all the time that they love things that will leave - no, better, things that are already leaving. You possess whatever is given by Fortune without a guarantor." (Seneca, Consolation to Marcia)

If an evil has been pondered beforehand, the blow is gentle when it comes. To the fool, however, and to him who trusts in fortune, each event as it arrives "comes in a new and sudden form," and a large part of evil, to the inexperienced, consists in its novelty. This is proved by the fact that men endure with greater courage, when they have once become accustomed to them, the things which they had at first regarded as hardships. (Seneca, Letter 76)

It is important to regularly spend time meditating on the worst outcomes you can possibly imagine. Spend 10 minutes imagining losing your sight in an accident. Your child to a disease. Your livelihood and reputation in one dramatic melt-down. Your life.

Whatever you are currently most afraid of, whatever has been haunting your thoughts - that.

Do it for 10 minutes. For 10 whole minutes, walk through each agonizing step of your excruciating loss. What would you do? How would you handle it? Could you really be "Stoic" about it? Possibly not.

But in ten minutes, you'll open your eyes and all will be as it was. None of your worst fears will have happened.

Only, now, you will have faced those fears and know that you will get past them, one way or another. If it happens, you will not be debilitated with shock. You will get to work on what comes next. You will appreciate what you have, and yet fully accept that it is only yours so long as Lady Luck wills it.

You will be stronger versus that which you fear the most.

It sounds horrible and morbid. It sounds like a nasty way to begin the day. But only by confronting your fears can you overcome them and learn to face whatever fate throws at you with serenity.

Retreat into the Self

People seek retreats for themselves in the countryside by the seashore, in the hills, and you too have made it your habit to long for that above all else. But this is altogether unphilosophical, when it is possible for you to retreat into yourself whenever you please; for nowhere can one retreat into greater peace or freedom from care than within one's own soul, especially when a person has such things within him that he merely has to look at them to recover from that moment perfect ease of mind (and by ease of mind I mean nothing other than having one's mind in good order). So constantly grant yourself this retreat and so renew yourself; but keep within you concise and basic precepts that will be enough, at first encounter, to cleanse you from all distress and to send you back without discontent to the life to which you will return. (Marcus Aurelius, Meditations 4.3)

How can you "get away from it all" when you always bring "it" with you? "It" is, of course, all your baggage. Your fears, your anxiety, your anger, your disappointment, your self-loathing, the lies you tell yourself, and the various poisons for which you lust. If that's what you want to get away from, there are cheaper tickets than the one at the airport.

The first thing you have to accept is that you cannot *buy* your peace of mind. And if you are trying to find it on a beach, you might as well stick your head in the sand and hum loudly to drown out your thoughts. If you want to see the world to broaden your horizons, that's all good, but the only place to go to fix your head is your head.

Try this exercise based upon work by Christopher Gill at Exeter: Next time you need some relief, find some quiet space. Go out to your car, if you must. Take a seat, close your eyes, and consider these facts:

- *Only your opinions, pursuits, desires, aversions, and actions are within your control. Nothing outside your control matters in your pursuit of peace.*
- *Nothing that happens to you can hurt you unless you choose to be hurt. It is only your own opinions of events that cause you to be disturbed.*

- *Change is natural and inevitable. You might as well get angry at the rain as be disturbed by change.*
- *Momento mori. The clock is ticking. What is the very next thing you will do to start moving in the right direction?*

Just those 4 things. Put them into your own words and make a mantra of them. Ponder them for as long as it takes and then get back to your work.

You have control over this. Even if you occasionally need to take a quick mental vacation to remember it.

Choose Your Company Well

Avoid fraternizing with non-philosophers. If you must, though, be careful not to sink to their level; because, you know, if a companion is dirty, his friends cannot help but get a little dirty too, no matter how clean they started out. (Epictetus, Enchiridion XXXIII.6)

Refuse the entertainments of strangers and the vulgar. (Epictetus, Enchiridion XXXIII)

Associate with people who are likely to improve you. (Seneca, Letter from a Stoic)

You can take this one as far as you will, but the point is simple: If you wallow with pigs, you're going to come out muddy. To the extent practical, you should surround yourself with people who use their heads. People who challenge you, and aren't entirely impressed with you. People who believe things you don't, and for good reason. People who make you wiser for having spent time in their company.

Conversely, avoid people who bring out your worst. People who drag you back into bad habits, who appeal to your baser instincts.

Jim Rohn says that everyone is an average of the five people they spend the most time with. If that's true, would you be okay with it?

Use Self-Deprecating Humor

If you learn that someone is speaking ill of you, don't try to defend yourself against the rumours; respond instead with, 'Yes, and he doesn't know the half of it, because he could have said more.' (Epictetus, Enchiridion XXXIII.9)

What a perfect way to deflate a verbal attack without climbing down into the mud pit. There's a skill to it, no doubt, but one that's easy enough to develop. Like everything else, you just have to practice. After a while, you'll have a few pat phrases and habits that make it impossible to put you down.

Self-deprecation is a gentle way of showing that your self-esteem is strong enough to take a beating without losing your sense of humor. With every insult, you appear stronger. Your very willingness to accept barbs and one-up them shows how far off the mark they must be.

And best of all, there is no escalation. No excuse for further animosity. You *agreed* with the harsh assessment, and even piled more onto it. What more can be said against you? What point is there in further assaults?

There is nothing like showing you can take a punch to suck all the fun out of throwing one.

Let the Other Guy Talk

In your conversation, don't dwell at excessive length on your own deeds or adventures. Just because you enjoy recounting your exploits doesn't mean that others derive the same pleasure from hearing about them. (Epictetus - Enchiridion XXXIII.14)

So, yeah, no one wants to hear your war stories. Or, they might, but they'll generally ask if they do. Otherwise, you can assume that they are far more interested in sharing *their* deeds of amazing adventure. And that's okay.

Spending time talking about yourself is both boring and useless. The most boring guy you know does this all the time. Always talking about how rich he is, or how crafty he is, or how good he is with the ladies, or how much fun he has. You hate that guy. Don't be that guy.

Furthermore, going on about your glory days does virtually nothing to help you. You aren't learning anything. You aren't helping the conversation move along. You aren't even convincing your associates of your conversational skills. You're just boring people.

So let the other guy tell his stories. They might be entertaining. They might tell you something about him he might not otherwise share. Or, it might just make him think you are pretty cool for listening.

Live Simply

Is it not madness and the wildest lunacy to desire so much when you can hold so little? ... [it is folly] to think that it is the amount of money and not the state of mind that matters! (Seneca, Consolation to Helvia)

For my part, I would choose sickness rather than luxury, for sickness harms only the body, but luxury destroys both body and soul. Luxury induces weakness in the body, cowardice and lack of self-control in the soul; and further it begets injustice and covetousness in others, and in self the failure in one's duty to friends, city and the gods. ... So, then, as being the cause of injustice, luxury and extravagance must be shunned in every way. (Musonius Rufus, Lecture XVIIIb)

It can seem natural to want the finer things in life, possibly because practically everyone does. Who wouldn't want a bigger house, a faster car, or a more exotic vacation? Don't *haute cuisine* and fine wine simply *taste* better than pizza and cheap beer?

But the fact that something serves its purpose well doesn't mean that it serves yours. Your purpose in life is not to consume the best of all things. Yours is to achieve *arete'* - fulfillment through excellence of character.

The pursuit of luxury precludes the pursuit of virtue. You can't focus on both. The possession of luxury creates a mental attachment to the ephemeral, to things outside ourselves and our control. The consumption of luxury becomes a dangerous step upon the hedonic treadmill and a never-ending need for more and more.

The "good life", then, is anything but. The material objects and powerful sensations that so many believe to be the epitome of success are, instead, self-inflicted obstacles that prevent it. The *wise* man would seek to purge from his life everything that does not contribute to his goals, because anything that isn't helping is at best a distraction.

Perfection is achieved not when there is nothing more to add, but rather when there is nothing more to take away. (Antoine de Saint-Exupry)

Everything of value you can ever hope to possess will exist within you. Your wisdom. Your courage. Your sense of justice. Your self-discipline. Anything else is just noise and baggage.

Speak Without Judging

Someone bathes in haste; don't say he bathes badly, but in haste. Someone drinks a lot of wine; don't say he drinks badly, but a lot. Until you know their reasons, how do you know that their actions are vicious? This will save you from perceiving one thing clearly, but then assenting to something different. (Epictetus, Enchiridion XLV)

One must persistently work on viewing the world as objectively as feasible. This aids in reducing the impact of our initial impressions which, in turn, aids us in avoiding unwise reactions. To that end, it's useful to develop the habit of, as much as possible, removing opinion and hyperbole from our observations, both mental and verbal.

If you see someone you might be inclined to judge as overweight, think instead of their exact weight, which is a fact, rather than the judgment that there is too much of it. Better yet, see them as a whole person, with all their objective characteristics rather than one you would single out.

If the weather strikes you as hot, focus instead on the temperature. If your back is killing you, think that there is a sharp sensation. If your boss is overbearing, think instead that he appears to care deeply about the topic. You are in no position to judge if he cares "too much".

The judgment adds nothing but unhelpful emotion. See the world as it is and work from that.

Educate by Example

On no occasion call yourself a philosopher, nor talk at large of your principles among the multitude, but act on your principles. For instance, at a banquet do not say how one ought to eat, but eat as you ought. (Epictetus, Enchiridion XLVI)

If you wish to help others find virtue, telling them about the great Truth you have found, the one they *didn't* find, is perhaps the least effective way to do it. It's arrogant and positions you as some kind of enlightened guru with private access to wisdom with others as mere acolytes at your feet

The wisdom of your "teachings" is not as readily apparent coming out of your mouth as it would be when derived from your character. If you want people to be less rancorous, communicate without rancor. If you want to teach them how to avoid letting their emotions overcome them, be a Zen chill dude. And if you want to teach them the wisdom of applied silence, shut up.

... if any conversation should arise among uninstructed persons about any theorem, generally be silent; for there is great danger that you will immediately vomit up what you have not digested. And when a man shall say to you that you know nothing, and you are not vexed, then be sure that you have begun the work (of philosophy). For even sheep do not vomit up their grass and show to the shepherds how much they have eaten; but when they have internally digested the pasture, they produce externally wool and milk. Do you also show not your theorems to the uninstructed, but show the acts which come from their digestion.
(Epictetus, Enchiridion XLVI)

If you derive your happiness from your own virtue, then you have no need to convince others of your wisdom. If you consider it your duty to share what you've learned, understand that an unwilling audience is unlikely to benefit from your efforts. If they perceive you are wise, they will ask for your help. If they do not, you cannot force it on them, and any effort to do so will only prove you aren't as smart as you think you are.

By focusing on your own actions, you strengthen your virtue and set a good example for others. You avoid pretentious pontification and irritated egos. And you make your point in the only way you effectively can.

Practice Discomfort

Set aside a certain number of days during which you shall be content with the scantiest and cheapest fare, with coarse and rough dress, saying to yourself the while, 'Is this the condition that I feared?' (Seneca, Letters, 18)

Difficulties strengthen the mind, as labour does the body. (Seneca, Morals)

Resilience is a huge part of Stoic practical philosophy. The idea is that intentionally subjecting one's self to inconvenience and minor pains will prepare you to better withstand the challenges of the real thing with equanimity. Stoics (and other Greek schools of philosophy) would famously do things like hug cold statues in the morning or walk about in uncomfortable clothing to build mental scar tissue. If one could develop the habit of dismissing minor annoyances as "indifferents" of no consequence, how much harder would it be to dismiss major ones? To view them without dread?

The sage-in-training, then, should practice discomfort in minor ways whenever possible. Drink nothing but water one day, to temper one's will-power. Walk outside on a chilly day without the normal degree of layering to get a taste of what the weather feels like. Park on the other end of the parking lot and take the long way in. Turn the hot water down in the shower, or turn the AC off in the house. If you get an itch, metaphorical or otherwise, just let it be.

All of these little tests of the will strengthen it like a muscle and, hopefully, leave you fortified when the real test happens.

Seek Your Own Approval

Often I marvel at how men love themselves more than others while at the same time caring more about what others think of them than what they think of themselves. (Marcus Aurelius, Meditations Book XII)

If you ever happen to turn your attention to externals, so as to wish to please anyone, be assured that you have ruined your scheme of life. Be contented, then, in everything with being a philosopher; and, if you wish to be thought so likewise by anyone, appear so to yourself, and it will suffice you.
(Epictetus, Enchiridion 23)

It is amazing how willing people generally are to put their happiness, their sense of worth, and their peace of mind in the hands of others. They tell themselves that they cannot be happy unless that one loves them, or the other approves. They strive, in futility, to get the validation they crave from other people. They spend their whole lives wondering why others refuse to give them the acceptance they so desperately need to reach contentment.

They have chosen a path that simply does not lead where they want to go.

Eudemonia, that sense of fulfillment, of flourishing, that we all seek, is not something that someone else can give to us. It comes only from our own actions and judgments. It is the natural reward for virtuous acts - for living up to our standards and acting according to the values we hold dear. It is ours to have, at will, if we so choose to. We need only live our lives with as much wisdom as we can muster.

No one else can know what you have overcome to get where you are. They can't know if the efforts that lead to your outcomes were a triumph over adversity or a cake walk. Did you fight against temptation or phone it in? Did you stick to your values or do what was popular? Did you sweat and struggle to reach the finish line, or did it come naturally? Did you accomplish something meaningful to *you*, given *your* values and weaknesses, or did you just do something that looks good from the outside.

If you want happiness, you must stop looking for it in other people. Set your own standards for excellence and strive to meet them. There is nothing anyone else on the planet can do to help you reach that goal. And it's the only one that matters.

Enjoy the Silence

Let silence be your general rule; or say only what is necessary and in few words. We shall, however, when occasion demands, enter into discourse sparingly, avoiding such common topics as gladiators, horse-races, athletes; and the perpetual talk about food and drink. Above all avoid speaking of persons, either in the way of praise or blame, or comparison. (Epictetus, Enchiridion XXXIII)

When confronted with an uncomfortable pause in the conversation… let it be. When bored and reaching for something witty to say, just don't. There is nothing wrong with just letting the quiet stand.

I begin to speak only when I'm certain what I'll say isn't better left unsaid. (Cato the Younger)

In social settings where participation is to be expected, do *not*, of course, maintain a monkish muteness. It is out of place and possibly a cry for attention. Instead, be sure to answer all questions succinctly and with a smile, and to make the appropriate responses to grease the wheels of communication. Never let others hear a disparaging remark escape your lips, unless you want them to wonder how you speak in their absence. When it is your turn to broach a topic, make sure it is focused on anything but you and your obsessions. Try, "So what are you working on, now?", or "What are your thoughts on…", or maybe, "I noticed you have a new …".

And when your words come, let it be because they are missed. Let your words have the weight of being sparingly shared; of being well considered. Let them be pulled, rather than pushed.

Hold On Loosely

In the case of particular things that delight you, or benefit you, or to which you have grown attached, remind yourself of what they are. Start with things of little value. If it is china you like, for instance, say, 'I am fond of a piece of china.' When it breaks, then you won't be as disconcerted. When giving your wife or child a kiss, repeat to yourself, 'I am kissing a mortal.' Then you won't be so distraught if they are taken from you. (Epictetus, Enchiridion III)

This one's tough for a lot of people. It goes against much of what we are taught from birth about holding on tightly to those we love. But, to the Stoics, such attachments were plainly to, and subject to, things outside our control. You can, and even *should*, love the good people in your life, but you always must be prepared to carry on without them.

This exercise is similar to "Consider Worst Case Scenarios", above. Imagine the one who is closest to you, the one whom you would least like to live without, being irrevocably taken from you. Practice distancing yourself from the impulse to panic and grieve. That's not a requirement for appreciation. Now imagine yourself lovingly releasing them and accepting that, will it or fight it, fate has decided and you must carry on. How would you do so? What strengths would you need to bring to bear?

Never say of anything, "I have lost it"; but, "I have returned it." Is your child dead? It is returned. Is your wife dead? She is returned. Is your estate taken away? Well, and is not that likewise returned? "But he who took it away is a bad man." What difference is it to you who the giver assigns to take it back? While he gives it to you to possess, take care of it; but don't view it as your own, just as travelers view a hotel. (Epictetus, Enchiridion XXI)

Go through the practical steps in your mind. Funeral arrangements, divorce proceedings, account credentials, whatever is required. How would your life be different? What new responsibilities might you pick up, or activities might you cease?

Now consider what you might have said to them, how you might have treated them, had you more time. Well, consider yourself fortunate, because you do.

Renounce

The more of these things a man deprives himself of, or of other things like them, or even when he is deprived of any of them, the more patiently he endures the loss, just in the same degree he is a better man. (Marcus Aurelius, Meditations V.15)

It's not the daily increase but daily decrease. Hack away at the unessential.
(Bruce Lee)

You should regularly look to remove from your life that which you can do without. If possible, forever, but if not, at least for a while. Possessions, habits, hobbies, social commitments, whatever you can. Simplify your life so that there is less you can lose, less to weigh you down.

Likewise, of those things you cannot forever purge, at the very least try to occasionally do without. Skip the coffee for a week to reduce caffeine's grip on you. Skip your favorite shows so that you are not committed to keeping up with the soap opera. Turn off your phone one Sunday and remember how it felt to be offline.

None of these things are essential to your happiness. You already have what you need for that and it can't be taken away.

Focus on the Thing at Hand

Every moment, concentrate steadily as a citizen and a human being to do what you have before you with perfect and simple dignity, and feeling of affection, and freedom, and justice; and to put aside all else. And you will give yourself peace, if you do every act of your life as if it were the last, laying aside all carelessness and passionate aversion from the commands of reason, and all hypocrisy, and self-love, and discontent with the portion which has been given to you. You see how few the things are that, should you grab hold of them, you can to live a life which flows in quiet, and is like the existence of the gods; for the gods on their part will require nothing more from him who observes these things. (Marcus Aurelius, Meditations 2.5)

Buddhists have this concept of a thing called the "monkey mind". It's that chattering voice in your head that seems to pipe up whenever you set yourself to any task. It says things like, "I wonder if anyone has liked my Facebook post, yet" and "I bet there's a new article in my news feed now". When you wrestle it into grudging silence, it squirms and wriggles and waits for a moment of laxity to burst free and do a quick check of the Reddit front page. It simply must know what *else* is going on.

Mastering one's self is largely about mastering this tendency we have to skip from task to task, trying on our work like coats at a department store and waiting for one to grab our fancy. There is always something shinier right over there. And yet, if our mind is always on the next thing, then it is never on what we are actually doing. And if our mind is not engaged in the only moment where we exist, this one, then we might as well have never existed. We were never "there".

One should, instead, approach every task as if it mattered, as if it were important. Else, why have you chosen to do it? And if you have decided that a thing is to be done, then work at it as if it could be the very last impression you leave on this planet. Who knows what will happen next? If this was to be your last moment on Earth, would you want to spend it half-heartedly tending the garden of your life while checking your Twitter stream?

Better we should grasp every task we choose to do with both hands, and not let go until we have completed the work to our full satisfaction. Engage with the work - experience it. Live in the moment forcefully enough to remember it happened.

If Death comes while you are washing dishes, let him find you scrubbing them spotless. If he comes while you are driving to work, let him find you with both hands on the wheel. And, if he finds you in your bed, go with him satisfied that you have used your allotted minutes well.

Master Your Appetite

The man who eats more than he ought does wrong, and the man who eats in undue haste no less, and also the man who wallows in the pickles and sauces, and the man who prefers the sweeter foods to the more healthful ones, and the man who does not serve food of the same kind or amount to his guests as to himself.
(Musonius Rufus, On Food)

To the ancient Stoics, good health was nothing more than an "indifferent", albeit a preferred one. Being healthy was certainly better than being sickly, but was not a virtue in and of itself. The quest for six-pack abs and buns-of-steel was nothing but vanity, and did nothing for true fulfillment.

Mastering one's appetite is the very foundation of training in self-control.
(Musonius Rufus, On Food)

However, temperance was unquestionably a virtue, and it's opposite, gluttony, a vice. Those two qualities were instrumental in determining the manner in which an individual reacted to his impressions. A glutton would accept all impressions on presentation, without pausing to impose reason upon his reaction. If a slice of bacon appeared delicious, it would be eaten. If a portion of lima beans looked bland, it would be ignored.

How shameful it is to behave toward food in this way we may learn from the fact that we liken them to unreasoning animals rather than to intelligent human beings. (Musonius Rufus, On Food)

It is the reasoning faculty that sets us above the animals, and when we set it aside, its lack that makes us no better. Our reason allows us to analyze our initial impressions, and then assent or reject them. Because of our reason, we can objectively view the things we might initially desire, and decide whether taking them would actually be in our best interests. And we are at our best when we prevent our desires and aversions from overpowering our good sense.

It follows, then, that mastery of one's appetites is an essential step along the path toward mastery of one's entire life. If one is unable to cease from overeating, how can he learn to hold his tongue? If another will not eat her vegetables, will she be able to perform her duty?

And, so, daily we must prepare to battle our appetites. And some days, we will lose. No matter - the battle itself makes us stronger, so long as we never quit trying. Self-mastery is not a state one achieves. It is a skill one hones.

Break It Down

When we have meat before us and such eatables, we receive the impression that this is the dead body of a fish, and this is the dead body of a bird or of a pig; and again, that this Falernian is only a little grape juice, and this purple robe some sheep's wool dyed with the blood of a shellfish; or, in the matter of sexual intercourse, that it is merely an internal attrition and the spasmodic expulsion of semen: such then are these impressions, and they reach the things themselves and penetrate them, and so we see the things as they truly are. Just in the same way ought we to act all through life, and where there are things that appear most worthy of our approbation, we ought to lay them bare and look at their worthlessness and strip them of all the words by which they are exalted. For outward show is a wonderful perverter of reason, and when you are most sure that you are employed about things worth your pains, it is then that it cheats you most.
(Marcus Aurelius, Meditations VI.13)

In any situation, during any struggle, when faced with any overpowering experience, break whatever it is down into its smallest components. So much of our initial reaction is based upon what we have brought to the situation, rather than the situation itself. Brush off the dross to find the truth beneath.

If you are facing an insurmountable problem, ask yourself what you are really looking for. Maybe it's as simple as the very next step that is doable right now. Once that's behind you, the seemingly insurmountable problem is already on its way to solution.

If you are facing an overpowering emotional response, ask yourself what has, at its most basic level, happened. Perhaps someone has been rude to you. Once you peel away the hurt pride and silly indignation, perhaps it's just a sad little person trying to save face. So, what of it?

When overcome with attachment to a thing, dig down deeply into whatever commands your emotions. Is it a toy, a trinket, you can simply live without? A bit of metal and plastic representing a few hours work and a new life-lesson? Is it truly deserving of your emotion?

Stripped of the drama and passion we seem to apply so liberally, most situations end up looking rather small.

Emulate Your Role Models

We need to set our affections on some good man and keep him constantly before our eyes, so that we may live as if he were watching us and do everything as if he saw what we were doing. (Seneca, Letters, 65)

When you are going to confer with anyone, and especially with one who seems your superior, represent to yourself how Socrates or Zeno would behave in such a case, and you will not be at a loss to meet properly whatever may occur. (Epictetus, Enchiridion XXXIII)

Similarly to how Marcus Aurelius begins his "Meditations", and almost the completely opposite of his thoughts under the "Brace for Trolls" heading, one might find it uplifting and inspirational to consider those traits in others they admire the most. Contemplating an actual role model, a real person, who has "nailed" a virtue is one way to help get better at it yourself. It underlines the point that the excellence to which you strive *can*, in fact, be achieved by actual humans.

If anything is possible for man, and peculiar to him, think that this can be attained by thee. (Marcus Aurelius, Meditations VI.19)

There is, perhaps, an added bonus in lessening one's cynicism. It's so easy to find the worst in others, one needs regular reminders that there is more to them. It's hard to work towards your purpose when you wallow in hopelessness.

Do not be discouraged that your role models have failed in other ways. We all do. That's what makes their achievements attainable for the rest of us. Admire them for what they have accomplished, and integrate their methods, the ones that work, into your own.

Try to act in the manner you would imagine your role models would until it is no longer an act.

Turn It Around

When you are offended at any man's fault, immediately turn to yourself and reflect in what manner you yourself have erred: for example, in thinking that money is a good thing or pleasure, or a bit of reputation, and the like. (Marcus Aurelius, Meditations X.30)

Practice this exercise when you feel the urge to judge another. The faults of others are not your concern. They don't impact anything important in you, and their correction is not under your control. Further, you are not free of fault yourself.

He that is without sin among you, let him first cast a stone... (Jesus of Nazareth, KJV John 8:7)

In many situations, with a little reflection, you will find an error on your own part that has contributed to any conflict you might be experiencing. If you are not in conflict, the fact that you have put yourself forward as the judge of another, without knowing all that has led them to where they are, is fault enough to consider. It is also likely that you have, yourself, been tempted to act in a similar manner. You may have on occasion even given in to it.

Your only concern is to improve the faults within yourself. The only interest you should take in the "faults" of others is to see if there is in them some lesson for you.

Take a View from Above

You can rid yourself of many useless things among those that disturb you, for they lie entirely in your imagination; and you will then gain for yourself ample space by comprehending the whole universe in your mind, and by contemplating the eternity of time, and observing the rapid change of every part of everything, how short is the time from birth to dissolution, and the illimitable time before birth as well as the equally boundless time after dissolution. (Marcus Aurelius, Meditations IX.32)

This is an exercise aimed at helping you maintain perspective. So much of what vexes us only has significance because we have chosen to *give* it significance. Remembering where we and our petty concerns fit into the global scheme of things may change how we view our challenges.

Wherever you are, close your eyes and picture yourself from outside. The way you are dressed, how you are positioned, your immediate surroundings. With your eyes still closed, pull back and take in the area around you and the other people nearby. Continue the exercise, pulling further away, but keeping "you" in the center. Take in the nearby streets and buildings, then those further away.

Now, imagine that you are zooming in and out, watching everyone around you. People sleeping, people working, people having first kisses, and people saying goodbye. People experiencing triumph, and people going through tragedy. First days on the job, unexpected terminations, car wrecks and marathon finishes. The entirety of the human experience happening in one instant, all around you.

After holding all of that in your mind for a moment, it's hard to remember what you thought was such a big deal before.

Own It

When you have decided that a thing ought to be done, and are doing it, never avoid being seen doing it, though the many shall form an unfavorable opinion about it. For if it is not right to do it, avoid doing the thing; but if it is right, why are you afraid of those who shall find fault wrongly? (Epictetus, Enchiridion XXXV)

Sometimes, acting according to your values can make you feel like a putz. All the cool kids are doing... whatever is currently cool, and here you are, following your silly principles. It's enough to make one want to slip off to the side and be principled in private.

However, this would, in itself, be a failure of the Stoic precept that only virtue matters. Your reputation with the in-crowd is a definite "indifferent", and a principled person would not sacrifice virtue for something that simply doesn't matter.

Anything done according to your values is worth doing openly. Perhaps others will see your example and learn from it. Perhaps your skin will grow a little thicker.

And anything that must be done in secret is better not done at all. If an act is both a vice and an embarrassment, there is simply no justification for it.

Walk in Your Enemy's Shoes

Let us put ourselves in the place of him with whom we are angry. At present an overweening conceit of our own importance makes us prone to anger, and we are quite willing to do to others what we cannot endure to be done to ourselves.
(Seneca, On Anger, 3.12)

When people injure you, ask yourself what good or harm they thought would come of it. If you understand that, you'll feel sympathy rather than outrage or anger. Your sense of good and evil may be the same as theirs, or near it, in which case you have to excuse them. Or your sense of good and evil may differ from theirs. In which case they're misguided and deserve your compassion. Is that so hard?
(Marcus Aurelius, Meditation Book VII)

It's common to imagine that when someone makes us angry, their actions were about us. That they either intended to wrong us or, at best, did so out of negligence. But any misdeed, if it exists, is only their logical (from their vantage) response to their own circumstances. We are, at most, a bystander.

When any person does ill by you, or speaks ill of you, remember that he acts or speaks from an impression that it is right for him to do so. Now it is not possible that he should follow what appears right to you, but only what appears so to himself. Therefore, if he judges from false appearances, he is the person hurt, since he, too, is the person deceived. (Epictetus, Enchiridion XLII)

When you feel another has treated you unkindly, unfairly, thoughtlessly, or in any way you would understand to be in error, understand that they think the offending act is called for. They are quite possibly wrong, but it makes sense to them because they don't know better. Maybe they don't understand virtue like you do. Maybe they think there is something more important at stake. Maybe someone they trusted led them astray. If you took a moment to consider your impression of events, it shouldn't be too hard for you to imagine a plausible sequence of events that might lead you to act the same way.

We are all the products of our past; our genetics and experience. Yours now includes the capacity to consider events objectively, and from the viewpoint of another. You can dismiss the irrelevant details of your bruised ego or marginally reduced circumstances to see the misfortune of the person who struggles in ignorance and confusion. You have full control over how you will respond.

It shouldn't take much effort to realize that you are the fortunate one in this encounter.

Nail Your Part

Remember that you are an actor in a drama, of such a kind as the author pleases to make it. If short, of a short one; if long, of a long one. If it is his pleasure you should act a poor man, a cripple, a governor, or a private person, see that you act it naturally. For this is your business, to act well the character assigned you; to choose it is another's. (Epictetus, Endichirion 17)

Fate has chosen a role for you. It is the role you fill right now. It is comprised of all your weaknesses, strengths, wisdom and ignorance. It includes the responsibilities you have accrued up to now, and all the debts owed to you, or by you. The entire chain of causality back to the beginning of time has conspired to place you into the role you fill at this moment in time.

What will you do, now?

The correct answer is, "My job, as best I can."

It is irrelevant how ill-prepared you feel you might be for the challenges you face. It simply doesn't matter if you don't want the role you find yourself playing. That's the one you have. You can fill that role well or you can do so poorly, but you will fill it regardless.

Reflect on the other social roles you play. If you are a council member, consider what a council member should do. If you are young, what does being young mean, if you are old, what does age imply, if you are a father, what does fatherhood entail? Each of our titles, when reflected upon, suggests the acts appropriate to it. (Epictetus, Discourses II)

One seeking wisdom will analyze his life objectively, and take honest inventory of his roles; as a parent, a student, an employee, a leader - whatever those roles might be. For some roles, the only virtuous path is to leave them. For others, it is to endure them. A prisoner, a patient and an exile each have their own opportunities for excellence. The role itself is unimportant, to be neither desired nor feared. The role is not the person. It is simply part of the environment in which they must act.

The world is filled with children who whine and complain bitterly about the roles thrust upon them, as if the universe should, somehow, bend reality to pave a more gentle path for them. You should, instead, seek to be the adult in the room, the calm voice of practicality who notes that, fairness aside, here we are. All that matters is what we do next.

Reconsider the Wrong

If any man has done wrong, the harm is his own. But perhaps he has not done wrong.
(Marcus Aurelius, Meditations IX.38)

When faced with an impression of wrongdoing, consider the possibility that it's just your perspective that makes it appear so. What if there is more to the situation than is initially apparent? What if there are extenuating circumstances?

It is important to remember that everyone acts from the facts and circumstances presented to them by fate. From their vantage, their acts seem to be rational, even imperative. Just because it looks different from yours does not mean that *they* should have acted differently.

You are never privy to the full story. You cannot know the entirety of another's motivations. You don't know his burdens, his fears, his pain.

Steven Covey tells a story in his "7 Habits" series about a man who entered a subway car with a pack of unruly children. They were yelling back and forth, throwing things, even grabbing people's papers, while the father just stared off into the distance. Covey was so disturbed by his apparent disinterest in controlling his children, and so irritated by their behavior, he was compelled to confront the man and bring it to his attention. The man admitted his failure, noting that their mother had just died an hour ago and no one knew quite what to do with themselves.

Covey's "impression of wrongdoing" was immediately adjusted.

You cannot walk another's path. You are in no position to judge his fault. Rather than wasting energy on being offended and scandalized, consider instead your own imperfections. These, at least, are not hidden from you.

Police Your Thoughts

There are four principal aberrations of the superior faculty against which you should be constantly on your guard, and when you have detected them, you should wipe them out and say on each occasion thus: this thought is not necessary; this tends to destroy social union; this which you are going to say comes not from the real thoughts — for you should consider it among the most absurd of things for a man not to speak from his real thoughts. But the fourth is when you shall reproach yourself for anything, for this is an evidence of the diviner part within you being overpowered and yielding to the less honorable and to the perishable part, the body, and to its gross pleasures. (Marcus Aurelius, Meditations XI.19)

Objective thinking comes from reviewing one's own thoughts as if they were separate from the thinker. It is this very act of viewing them as standalone objects that allows us to reject those thoughts that are not fit for purpose. In this way, we select the thoughts according to our values, rather than allowing our values to be shaped by whatever comes to us. Thoughts must be seen as tools that help us become what we strive for, rather than indicators of who we are.

Some thoughts are not helpful in the moment. Some distract us or tempt us or take us off course. Some are needlessly hurtful, or are untrue or insincere. What you consider to be an unworthy thought is entirely up to you and your individual path, but the key is that you make a habit of challenging what is going on within your own head. It is more important to be right than to adhere to your "convictions".

Convictions are more dangerous foes of truth than lies. (Friedrich Nietzsche, Human All Too Human)

Do your thoughts align with your values? If not, reject them and reach for better ones.

Amor Fati

Don't demand that things happen as you wish, but wish that they happen as they do happen, and you will go on well. (Epictetus, Enchiridion 8)

Fate leads the willing and drags along the reluctant. (Seneca, Letters to Lucilius)

My formula for what is great in mankind is amor fati: *not to wish for anything other than that which is; whether behind, ahead, or for all eternity. Not just to put up with the inevitable – much less to hide it from oneself, for all idealism is lying to oneself in the face of the necessary – but to love it.* (Nietzsche, Ecce Homo, 10)

When the philosophers talk about *Amor Fati*, "Love your fate", they mean the bad parts. There's no difficulty in loving your fate when you've just won the lottery. For most people, it should be relatively easy to grasp why we should *accept* our fate. It's going to happen, so why fight the unavoidable? It is far more difficult to understand, however, why we should "love" it. It seems Stoic enough if we can just "grin and bear it", right?

Well, no. It's not enough. I suppose it's better than whining about how the world is out to get us, but ideally, life is a lot better once we learn to truly *love* the "opportunities for excellence" the universe presents to us.

Fate, in the form of the challenges it incessantly spawns, is what makes us strong. A universe in which we do not need to overcome challenge, where we do not actively seek it, is one where we grow weak and our lives are bland and ordinary. Our daily struggles are what gives us backbone. Every time we get rained on, or fired, or insulted, or robbed, we get a chance to respond with virtue. And, if we do, we gain resilience, fortitude, and wisdom.

The manner in which we respond to our fate becomes the foundation of our character. If anything determines who we become, it is this interaction. And to be great, to be someone worthy of our own respect, we need a great adversary against which to spar and test ourselves.

And so we learn to actually *love* our fate, not merely to bear it. We love it because it makes us better. We love it because, without it, who would we be?

Write It Down

The spirit ought to be brought up for examination daily. It was the custom of Sextius when the day was over, and he had betaken himself to rest, to inquire of his spirit: 'What bad habit of yours have you cured to-day? What vice have you checked? In what respect are you better?' (Seneca, On Anger III.36)

Another form of "Reviewing Your Impressions" is keeping a journal. Much as Marcus Aurelius did with his Meditations, you may find it helpful to reflect upon the day's happenings and your impressions thereof in print. That adds a little weight to the process, and encourages a deeper form of reflection. It creates a record for you to review periodically, to pinpoint trends, noting lessons you have trouble keeping in mind. It also provides suggestions and inspirations from the "past" you that might help with current challenges. You and he, after all, have a lot in common.

It's another opportunity for emotional housekeeping.

Memento Mori

Acquire the contemplative way of seeing how all things change into one another, and constantly attend to it, and exercise yourself about this part of philosophy. For nothing is so much adapted to produce magnanimity. … Consider in what condition both in body and soul a man should be when he is overtaken by death; and consider the shortness of life, the boundless abyss of time past and future, the feebleness of all matter. (Marcus Aurelius, Meditations X.11)

What wouldst thou be found doing when overtaken by Death? If I might choose, I would be found doing some deed of true humanity, of wide import, beneficent and noble. But if I may not be found engaged in aught so lofty, let me hope at least for this—what none may hinder, what is surely in my power—that I may be found raising up in myself that which had fallen; learning to deal more wisely with the things of sense; working out my own tranquility, and thus rendering that which is its due to every relation of life. (Epictetus, Golden Sayings:189)

Death can come at any time. What that means is that all of the wonderful things you plan on doing this weekend, when your kids graduate, when you retire - It's entirely possible that none of that will happen. If you're living your life for the future, you just might be wasting it.

Thinking about the inevitability of your death, and on the unpredictable timing of it, can't help but emphasize the importance of living in the "here and now". You cannot hold off doing the right thing until it is more convenient because it might never happen. You cannot hold off doing the things that fulfill you until you have more time because you may already be out of it.

You have a 100% chance of doing whatever you are doing right now. Nothing more is guaranteed.

Review the Day

Never allow sleep to close your eyelids, after you went to bed,

Until you have examined all your actions of the day by your reason.

In what have I done wrong? What have I done? What have I omitted that I ought to have done?

If in this examination you find that you have done wrong, reprove yourself severely for it;

And if you have done any good, rejoice.

Practise thoroughly all these things; meditate on them well; you ought to love them with all your heart.

It is those that will put you in the way of divine virtue. (The Golden Verses of Pythagoras)

At the end of the day, shortly before you go to bed, set some time aside to review how well you handled the day's challenges. Were you faithful to your principles? Did you lose your temper? Did you perform your duties, as you understand them, diligently? What vices did you give in to, and how will you handle them differently tomorrow? What lessons have you learned that you'll need to apply going forward?

Put a capstone on your day. Take (a little) pride in the courage you showed, sticking to your values when it was hard. Resolve to do better where your self-discipline was weak. Nod off secure in the knowledge that you've gained a little more wisdom with which to face your next day's challenges.

A Final Word

How long are you going to wait before you demand the best for yourself and in no instance bypass the discriminations of reason? You have been given the principles that you ought to endorse, and you have endorsed them. What kind of teacher, then, are you still waiting for in order to refer your self-improvement to him? You are no longer a boy but a full-grown man. If you are careless and lazy now and keep putting things off and always deferring the day after which you will attend to yourself, you will not notice that you are making no progress but you will live and die as someone quite ordinary. From now on, then, resolve to live as a grown-up who is making progress, and make whatever you think best a law that you never set aside. And whenever you encounter anything that is difficult or pleasurable or highly or lowly regarded, remember that the contest is now, you are at the Olympic games, you cannot wait any longer, and that your progress is wrecked or preserved by a single day and a single event. This is how Socrates fulfilled himself by attending to nothing except reason in everything he encountered. And you, although you are not yet Socrates, should live as someone who at least wants to be Socrates. (Epictetus, Enchiridion LI)

Without the action to back it, a philosophy is just a lazy intellectual exercise. A philosophy is not a puzzle to be unwound and put aside. It is a guide for daily living and, for it to have any worth, it must be lived. Do not wait for perfect understanding. Do not wait for the ideal opportunity. If you believe this is important, it is important enough to do right here and right now.

As Marcus Aurelius said, "Stop philosophizing about what a good man is and be one."

The End

For comments, questions, and corrections, you can find me at /u/GreyFreeman on Reddit or my own blog at http://c0c0c0.net.

Acknowledgements

Many thanks to Massimo Pigliucci at "How to Be a Stoic" whose essays on practical Stoicism provided the initial inspiration for this booklet.

Thanks also to the r/Stoicism community on Reddit for their support in the editing this booklet.

Appendix: Companion Material

As noted at the beginning of this booklet, "Practical Stoicism" is not, in itself, a solid introduction into Stoicism. At its heart, it is something I simply wrote for myself to keep me focused on those actions I should be integrating into my daily existence. For any of this to make coherent sense, however, it is essential to bone up on the thinking that went into these practices. For that, you need something structured a little differently. Here are some suggestions on where to start.

The Stoic Handbook by Erik Wiegardt

The good folks at the "The College of Stoic Philosophers" put this short PDF together for the expressed purpose of introducing western readers to the philosophy. It's written in plain, straightforward English and lays out the basics concepts in about as obvious a manner as you could hope. Free (http://collegeofstoicphilosophers.org/books/10).

Stoicism and the Art of Happiness by Donald Robertson

This book follows a similar modernistic model as *"The Stoic Handbook"*, but goes a little deeper. The author is a psychotherapist of the Stoic-Inspired CBT method and you can see it in the scientific references he brings to bear in explaining why the philosophy works. Nor does he skimp on the history behind each of the principles he discusses. Complete with exercises at the end of each chapter to help you start seeing how the whole thing fits together, this is an excellent way to get started. Around $14 for the paperback on Amazon (http://www.amazon.com/Stoicism-Art-Happiness-Teach-Yourself/dp/1444187104).

Enchiridion by Epictetus

"Enchiridion" literally translates to "Handbook" and was compiled by Epictetus' students from the larger body of his "Discourses" for the expressed purpose of introducing the *prokopton* (one who is making moral progress) to the essentials of Stoicism. I started with the George Long translation, one of the more popular ones, but that's largely because it is no longer under copyright. There are more recent translations of this, and many other older Stoic writings, and some would argue that a nominal charge is worth the additional clarity. Your mileage may vary. Free from Wikisource (https://en.wikisource.org/wiki/Enchiridion_(Epictetus)).

While I mention *Meditations* and various other writings throughout this booklet, I would *not* consider those to be ideal introductory pieces. They were not meant to be an introduction to this philosophy, and were not structured as such. If, upon reading the basics laid out in a manner that attempts to lead you logically from premise to conclusion you want to go deeper, there is a large and growing body of work to take you there. For that, I would direct you to the "Resources" section of the Reddit Stoicism FAQ (https://www.reddit.com/r/Stoicism/wiki/faq), which offers a number of suggestions with brief descriptions of each.

Finally, be sure to check out the original conversations surrounding this booklet at Reddit/r/Stoicism (https://www.reddit.com/r/Stoicism/comments/4bz797/practical_stoicism/).

About the Author

"Grey Freeman" is the pen name behind which the author hides all his hobbies, obsessions and bad habits. He is, literally, just a guy on the internet, and claims no special credentials or divine knowledge. The most interesting thing about him is his amused acceptance of the fact that he isn't all that interesting.

Made in the USA
Coppell, TX
24 May 2021